"No matter who you work for, always work for yourself. Don't think for a minute that the company you work for has your best interest at heart more than you should or do."

H. G. Grinter, Sr.

The Art of Working for Yourself

No Matter Who You Work For
How to Always Work for Yourself

Authored by H. Gerald Grinter

The Art of Working for Yourself

ISBN-10: 0985536101

ISBN-13: 9780985536107

DEDICATION

I would like to dedicate this book to the five people in my life who have helped me navigate this journey and allowed me to bring this book to you. Without them all of this would not have been possible. The first two are Howard and Patricia Grinter. I am forever grateful for your incredible guidance and helping hands along the journey of my life. From the stories and laughter to the discipline I needed to keep me on the right path when I strayed. Thank you mom and dad for EVERYTHING! Don Burrows, sir, you are the greatest thing since sliced bread. Thank you from the bottom of my heart, for blowing the dust off of the cover of my life and shining a light on my soul and helping me be the meatball in the spaghetti. And Deborah Drake, lady, you are my angel that allowed me to see who I truly am and know it's okay for me to be me. You helped me find my voice and taught me how to share it with the world.

Last but not least I would like to thank everyone else in my life as a collective soul that wrapped their arms around me when I needed it and pushed me when it was necessary. Mere words could never express how much your support means to me. I love you all.

CONTENTS

INTRODUCTION

It was a January afternoon. My view spectacular as always was this day, rainy, overcast and cold, as I called my father from my office. I remember looking out of my window thinking to myself, "How I could not enjoy this time in my life. I'm on the 42nd floor with a window office overlooking the Puget Sound. People work their whole lives for an office with a view like this one, and yet there I was having what felt like the worst day possible.

In truth, it was like any other day: Client calls, a little customer "TLC" and a few new proposals in the bag. Yet, I was on the verge of tears not understanding why I felt the way I did.

I feel like I fell off the proverbial "entrepreneur/business owner" apple cart, by way of my father's insurance agency in my youth, where I would file odd papers and occasionally accompany him to take pictures of homes and businesses he would insure. Reflecting now, on then, some part of me already knew one day I'd be working for myself.

So on this chaotic day, not understanding why I was so unhappy, I called the one person I knew would understand, my father. I remember when he started his agency in the basement of our house. Yes, the basement. Some 25 years later he sold it after my mother passed. His famous words to me when I was young have haunted me my whole life. He would say more than once, "Gerald, always work for yourself, remember that."

I didn't really understand what he meant until that late January afternoon as he was about to lay another stick of dynamite under my scalp--in the form of one of his world famous quotes. I never know where he gets them from, however he whips them out at always just the right time, knowing they will wreck your world for a few months thereafter. He always had impeccable timing.

So there I was, about to literally jump out of the window. My heart knew it was time to make a change and my ego wouldn't let me. I had just moved my office to this fantastic new address and things were about to get really nice. I had done all of things I was supposed to do to become successful. I courted the right clients, created a winning business mix, put all of the right systems in place, I was in the driver's seat and I was as unhappy as ever. Amidst my internal babbling my father says to me:

"There is nothing more tragic in life, than to climb the ladder of success only to find it has been leaned against the wrong wall."

I went home that night and grabbed a glass of my favorite wine and stood on my balcony in need of air. Was my ladder leaned up against the wrong wall? I was a business owner, working for myself, financially succeeding by most people's standards, and the reality had sunk in that I wasn't happy. I dreaded returning to work again another day doing something I was supposed to love.

I had chosen insurance because I knew it and that made it easy and over time the money would be good and my dad would be proud of me. But, in my heart of hearts I wanted to be elsewhere. As much as I love the game of business, I loved beautiful buildings. In hindsight, I see now I followed my dad in one way but not the other. He had his insurance business and had a couple of rental properties. I remember loving cutting the grass of those properties and everything else about making those buildings look a great as they did. I remember wishing I could spend hours just shaping the hedges. So why then did I choose the insurance route at the fork in the road?

And what gives me the right to tell my story? And, what does it mean to work for yourself?

I am an ordinary man who has lived an incredible life, accidentally as well as on purpose and managed not to kill myself in the process. I have had the opportunity to travel the world, learn different languages, and start, run and sell a successful business for more money than I could imagine and I believe I have learned a few things along the way about working for myself.

Although I didn't realized it at the time. I was always working for myself--sometimes more than others. In retrospect I see that I was mentally creating a game within the game wherever I worked. Thanks to my father's words, every time I got away from my core zone of working for myself, I knew it and I suffered until the universe kicked my butt back into shape.

Let me tell you a little bit about my father. We have all come across people who shape our lives and in some cases unknowingly. You meet them in the airport, they take the seat beside you on the bus and sometimes, they are a family member or a friend. They say what they say, do what they do, while we watch and then one day you find yourself transformed by your experience of them; your life is never the same for knowing them. Well, my father is that guy. He is a man of few words and yet has this insane ability to make his point crystal clear when he speaks to you. I hope to one day inherit his gift of words.

After selling my business I took some time away from the grind of life and gave myself the space to listen to my heart and watch others live and work through that lens. I simply watched and witnessed--as one who could slow down and choose what I wanted to do day by day. I also "worked" at a non-profit as a volunteer business mentor helping women and people in underserved communities start their own businesses to become self-sufficient.

It was during that time I re-discovered the art of working for yourself. It was in seeing through the eyes of those looking for something more professionally, something fulfilling, something they could call their own, something else of their creation that it all came into crystal clear focus for me.

Before you begin this book I have a few questions to ask you. Are you sure you know why you picked this book? You've read countless others like this and yet you chose this one. Why? Do you ever have that feeling like you are dreaming but you are awake while you work? Can you tell? We go through the motions of working and yet something doesn't feel quite right. For some it never has. Are you looking for a new way to work and live?

Here's the question to ask; "How can I work for someone else no matter who I work for?" It's questions like this that made you pick this book not just the answers you want. And this is where I will begin this book. I hope you enjoy reading it as much as I have enjoyed writing it.

"Sometimes in life all you need is 20 seconds of insane courage and I promise you something absolutely great will come of it." – "We Bought a Zoo" (The Movie)

CHAPTER ONE

Discovering the Art of Working for Yourself

I have decided to write this book after watching and listening to so many of my friends and colleagues talk about this world in which we live and how tough it is lately. How, many have lost their jobs and others who wish they had. There were friends of mine who knew it was only a matter of time before they were given their pink slips with massive layoffs happening around them. And oddly enough some of my friends who wanted to be let go, got offered attractive packages for positions half way across the country--that they didn't say no to. I think it is in these times we find ourselves and during these moments, taking an honest inventory is more important than ever.

The Art of Working for Yourself

According to the media and internet, more people have decided to start their own businesses these days than at any other time since the "Great Depression." I believe it. People are also giving the finger to major companies preferring to go it alone after being shown the corner office from one company or another and not liking what they see or how they were treated. In an effort to no longer work for "the man" or "the woman" they are burning their resumes and creating their own websites and business ventures. There are still a few souls out there that are still waiting for Superman to save the day. You probably know some of them. They come home every night thanking the universe that they still have a job or their business is still afloat.

All of this chaos and change takes me back to the memory of a fishing trip with my dad in Ohio. I was about 15 years old. It was a hot August afternoon and we were talking about me and my summer job at "Burger King." This was the first time I had ever worked for someone. You see as a youngster, I had a paper route for several years and when I was tired of that I took the customers I had and turned my paper route into a lawn cutting business--and I kept all my customers. So, I was used to doing pretty much what I wanted in the work arena. I began complaining to my dad about all of the things that my manager was asking me to do and the crazy hours I was working to make the same amount of money. My father looked at me and said the words that have stuck with me my whole life. "No matter who you work for, always work for yourself. Don't think for a minute that the company you work for will ever have your best interest at heart more than you do or should."

My first reaction was "What?" How can I work for myself when I am clearly under the employ of a "Burger King?" Needless to say I only worked there until the end of that summer. As much as I loved whoppers, it was tough working for someone else. It always has been for me. This brings me to my point. Is there an "Art to working for yourself?" I didn't know it at the time, but there truly is.

Back in high school, I was once fired or should I say "let go" from a job--for being too efficient. You see I have this knack for creating systems that allow me to work more efficiently, thus having as much down time as I want to do other things I want to do. While on the job I figured out how to finish all of my work by 11am (my shift started at 8am) and so I could watch TV, hang out in other parts of the building, so I could see what everyone else was doing or sleep for the rest of my shift. I thought I was brilliant until they called me in to the office and asked me if I wanted to resign or be fired. I resigned. Why didn't I see even back then, that I was not suited for working for someone else?

The Art of Working for Yourself

"No matter who you work for, always work for yourself. Don't think for a minute that the company you work for has your best interest at heart more than you should or do."

- H. G. Grinter, Sr.

Working for one's self is as much a mindset as it is a way of life. I'll explain. Most of us think that the only people who work for themselves are entrepreneurs who start their own business in their basement and take it to Fortune 500 status, then sell it and go live on the beach in Maui. Well, there is a little truth to this, but we've also worked with those who I call the bullet proof employee. We all have worked with someone like this at one time in our lives. They might be the slacker named Jason in the desk next to you who comes in just a little late, but not so late that they are fired for it, or the worker named Stacey who has the cleanest desk on earth and has this insane ability to be able to do all of her work and probably yours too if you asked her and leave at 5pm on the button--daring anyone to ask her to work a second of overtime or on the weekend.

I've often wondered how they managed to do this. And don't forget Jeff who is the boss's pet. He's the guy who manages to get first dibs on everything before the rest of the building even knows what's going on. They have all discovered the art of working for themselves.

It's the ability to take what you do and do it in such a way that it is done the way you want to do it, in your style and on your terms--within the space of the environment you are in.

I know this sounds like smoke and mirrors, but it's the truth. It's shaping the rules of the game to their style and requirements. So, while most of us are complaining about how our job sucks, they have figured out a way to focus on a much bigger goal: Their life and how they want to live it.

To do things the way you want to do them, you must first begin to think the way you want to think. This is the first step in understanding the art of working for yourself. If I could see your face right now, you probably have your head tilted to the side and are ready to give me your best "What you talkin' bout Willis"- (imagine my best Gary Coleman impression.)

You see for most of us, our opinions and attitudes and how we live our lives have been shaped by society, TV, crazy parents and our closest friends. We have had the individuality (and dare I suggest creativity) stomped out of us from the time we were very young and most of us still claim we think for ourselves. Okay, I may be going a bit far but you get my point. Sadly, some of us lose our natural childlike curiosity and drive sooner than others and restoring it is tougher work than we may imagine.

We live our lives according to what we've been told we should do--in order to not create the biggest waves. We've been talked out of our fondest hopes and dreams by well-meaning friends and family who laughed in our faces and made jokes about our dreams at our expense--just to get a laugh from the crowd. So we tuck these aspirations away in a corner of our hearts and pile all of life's other deferred dreams in front of and on top of them and mindlessly check out; taking the first option that comes along that makes us look good in everyone's eyes.

We then work at our jobs every day waiting for our retirement date to come like we're escaping from a maximum security prison. This is not working for yourself. And for many business owners who are a slave to the rhythm of the chaos--that is their business. Those of you who treat it like you are still working a nine-to-five job, you know who you are. You dread your business as much as you did going to work for the man or woman. I know what this looks like. It's time you learned the art of working for yourself too. Owning a business doesn't always mean you are working for yourself. Although you think you are. Okay, in theory you are, but there's more to it than simply owning the business itself. (Your business could own you if you aren't mindful.)

What we don't realize is that the companies we work for and the businesses we run have allowed us to suffer in comfort. I know this sounds rather extreme. But it's the truth. Think about how long you have gone without really getting what you want. And I don't mean that flat screen TV you just got for Christmas either. Let's talk about this, because this is where a lot of this begins. We have been spoon fed almost since birth our wants and desires through our media, our friends and families--and not once have we opened our mouth to express any form of individualism or heartfelt desire outside of our immediate basics needs. And if we do summon the courage to express something, it comes out in the form of a whisper as if we are tightening the bolt on a leaky faucet--trying to not let that drip escape again. Instead, we compete with one another in a race to see who can collect the most things, go on the coolest vacations, drive the best cars and get the closest to living the life of the rich and famous--all the while not really present in our lives and then later not sure how we ended up "here."

So how does this all work? How can you develop a mindset of working for your yourself? There are only a few steps needed to set upon this journey, and once you start, it will change your life. You will be able to truly say, no matter who you work for you can only work for yourself.

The Art of Working for Yourself

It truly starts with "DESIRE." I wish it was something more profound than this, but this is how and where it all begins. The art of working for yourself begins with wanting to work for yourself: No matter whom you work for. Taking in all the parameters you live and work with and creating in your heart a desire of what you want for your life. Now, it's not enough to just say "I want to work for myself." Anyone can do this. You have to actually define what you want your life to look like and how you plan to make this happen. Vague plans get you nowhere because there is no true path to follow. You must also create a definite picture in your heart and mind of what it's going to take to work for yourself and live your best life. The two need not be mutually exclusive. Then know how long it will take to get you there. This is where having a definite plan for your life is paramount. This will give you the power to foresee your future with incredible clarity. I know this sounds like a lot of work but it's not. Why? Because you've been dreaming of this moment all of your life, that's why. It's probably already been written and rewritten several times in your head since you were five years old. That's why! You just forgot.

Sure you've got some hard work ahead. But this pales in comparison to a life unfulfilled. Mountain climbers always talk about the last 100 feet being the toughest. Well, this is your last 100 feet. Changing your life isn't easy. If you desire to do something, then do it. Never mind what "they" say or if you stumble a few times. Every failure brings you closer to success.

You must plan all the way to the end, and in the greatest detail, taking into account everything that must be done to prepare yourself and any possible hindrances that may get in your way or slow you down. In creating your plan this way you won't be surprised by anything that appears and you'll know when and how to get around them.

This is the foundation of the "art of working for yourself" and this touch point will guide you towards the life you've always imagined.

"He who asks fortune tellers the future unwittingly forfeits an inner intimation of coming events that is a thousand times more exact than anything they may say."
-Walter Benjamin

So why write a plan at all, let alone in detail? Because most of us are so checked out that we need something like a plan to follow or we will fall back into our old lives. Most of us believe we've actually planned for the future because we've set up a mutual fund and have life insurance in case we die. Pause a moment and ask yourself, how does this sound? It sounds like you are waiting to die. Key word...waiting! We think we've planned ahead. This is in fact delusional thinking because we are using our vague desires and the stunted reality of our daily lives to envision our future as it should be. We have been taught to focus on the happily ever after and not the plan or the journey. By embracing the art of working for yourself you create for yourself a definite purpose backed with the desire to make it so.

Key Observations and Obstacles

Say what you want in defense of working for someone else or even working for yourself but no one can truly live a complete life unless he/she works for themselves. Why? Because you deserve it! I think most people naturally want to become all they are capable of becoming. Success in life is being all that you can be, expressing the full nature of who you are. There are no limitations to the mind except those we accept as our own. There are those of us who sit back and watch others hopes and dreams go up in smoke and give up--only to return to the plantation beaten and scared. But there a few, who take the "Clubber Lang" beat-down and come back like "Rocky Balboa" in the twelfth round. These are the ones who never accept life's challenges as the finish line, but more as the proving grounds to fine tune their desire and stoke the flames that sharpen their swords to cut a path and make their vision become real. This is what the art of working for yourself is made from.

"Few people take objectives really seriously. They put average effort into too many things, rather than superior thought and effort into a few important things. People who achieve the most are selective as well as determined."

- Richard Koch

CHAPTER TWO

What You Think About Matters

So, I bet you can tell I've been thinking about this for quite some time. It's been pretty much the chorus for most of my life. My father's words fading in and out in-between his many lectures on life. As I look back on things, I think I was sleep walking for a while. Checked out on life, just taking what life handed me. I think the way we think about and approach life has been handed down through the generations and primes us for how we live our own lives. From how we learn in school, to the friends we choose to the neighborhoods we live in. It all matters. The sad truth is, most of us don't really pay attention to what goes on around us (but it is never too late to start paying attention.)

Every dream we have, we shut down immediately not allowing ourselves the pleasure of having what we want, let alone thinking about the possibility of attaining it. What you think about matters. You must believe in what you want before you can impress upon the universe that desire that you will have it.

"Everything you need you already have. You are complete right now, you are a whole, total person, not an apprentice person on the way to someplace else. Your completeness must be understood by you and experienced in your thoughts as your own personal reality." - Beverly Sills

And here is where I start this chapter. You deserve to work for yourself: To live the life you've always wanted and dreamed possible. How is this possible you might ask, I work for someone else? Re-thinking what you do and how you do it, is how you start down this path.

Pay attention to what's going on around you. The signs are everywhere. There has been some incredible mind judo done to us by the mantras of the companies we work for, the television we watch and the company we keep. Every day we are bombarded with the distraction of comparing ourselves to each other instead of focusing on our own path in life. Stop and think about this. It's not about them. It's about you. You are the most important thing going. You always have been and always will be.

You can think for yourself. Most of us however fall short of thinking for ourselves because we are easily influenced by others, what they say and what they think about what we want. It's funny, when we tell others about our ideas, everyone has an opinion about how to do it and why it won't work or things we should look out for. It used to be all anyone had to do was laugh at something I said or express any type of dislike for my idea, and I would put my dream back into my pocket and take on their ideas as my own never to be mentioned again. I knew they all meant well. Okay, at least most of them.

When you have an idea to do something, be careful who you share it with--especially if it going against conventional thought or wisdom.

Sometimes we talk too much and don't listen to others or pay attention to what we are doing. Some will think you are showing off and others look forward to seeing you fail. I know this isn't the nicest thing to suggest, especially when it comes to our friends. Some of us don't even realize that our friends, family and acquaintances are the biggest obstacle keeping us where we are or where we want to go. This is something to be aware of as you begin "your" journey.

Some of your friends and family will not be able to come on this journey with you. My father lamented this to me as he was realizing his life changing the larger his insurance agency grew. He said, "It's sad to say this but sometimes in life your friends and colleagues have to change. You may not want them to, but they must. As you begin to change, so will how you look at things and them and sometimes they won't match and others will be waiting for you to join them."

Keep your eyes and ears wide open and your mouth occasionally closed. You know what they say. Those who say don't do and those who do don't say. Let your actions speak for you.

It's easy to get over-confident as we take inventory of our life and think we have it all together. Please, don't ever put anyone down and smash their dreams. I practice this with every fiber of my being and I am asking you to begin this practice too. I now ask this question before I say anything about someone's dreams or ideas—"What exactly is my motivation for commenting on another's aspirations? Do I need to make this person feel inferior in order to make myself feel better about myself?" Be honest with yourself! Asking questions is okay and giving constructive guidance is good. But, be nice and fair. Why rain on their parade?

Now, to begin this process for yourself, I will ask you to think back to when you were young and remember all of the things you always talked (or thought) about doing. I bet you have never forgotten them have you? I know I haven't. I'm still trying to do most of them today. This is where the art begins to come alive. This is where that gem of light shines brightest.

Thought is the only power which can produce the energy that gets you what you want.

What you think about matters. We have thoughts all of the time and yet we don't always honor them. Why not? We become paralyzed by the fear of not conforming or fitting in, to letting those voices of everyone we've ever known get in the way of what life is calling us to do. From buying that dress, to painting the garage floor, we second guess our actions. Most of us do. I've done it for years. I'll start by giving you a new phrase. We've all heard the acronym WWJD "What Would Jesus Do?" How about changing one letter and start by saying WWID "What Would I Do?" I am not trying to get really religious here, I'm just being creative.

Why is it our first instinct to defer to someone else when thinking about what we want or what we want to do—even before using our minds to think first about the situation and create a solution or outcome that we will be happy and satisfied with? It's as if we are waiting for some miracle to happen and everyone to agree. Why do we do this? I'll tell you why. That "passion muscle" has been neglected for years. Our natural drive to pursue what we want has been dampened by life's setbacks and the messages we've received growing up or it was blown out by the school bully thus creating a tactic of indecision in our hearts and minds. Take your pick. For most of us indecision has been fostered within us since we were young, becoming firmly rooted into our daily habits as we get older.

In fact for most of us we have followed a path chosen for us by someone else and carried this thinking into the careers that we've chosen--If in fact we chose our own career. Some of us blindly took the first or highest paying job that was offered because we had fallen into the habit of indecision. I would bet that about 95% of us have at some time or another have or currently work in a job they got because they couldn't figure out what to do. The knowledge of how to choose the career they desired was not known.

"Choose a job you love, and you will never have to work a day in your life." - Confucius

I believe conscious deliberate thought gives one confidence. It shapes your experiences and takes your mind to that creative space that believes anything is possible. Those who possess clearly defined thoughts and reach decisions quickly are thought of as someone knowing what they want and how to get it. Creating a conscious strength from within is another step toward developing the art of working for yourself. It keeps you from being satisfied with less than what you want or could attain. It is this type of consciousness that calls for increasing vitality in all you do. Sometimes this requires courage and focus and sometimes incredible courage we may not feel we have. But we do.

I will leave you with this. When you permit yourself to think about what is inferior in your life, your life becomes inferior and you will surround yourself with inferior things. The more you create an environment for great thoughts, the more good things you will have in your life. In the next chapter I will talk more about thoughts, thinking and wanting what others have.

Key Observations and Obstacles

If you haven't thought about being grateful, this is great place to start. I'm not telling you to go to the mountain top and starve yourself. I mean, in its simplest terms "be grateful." Grateful for where you are, grateful for everything you have and will experience in life. Just start there. Life is a journey as is working for yourself and none of us comes into life with infinite knowledge (that we can remember.) We begin where we are and build our ship as we go through life. Being grateful will get you in the habit of being in a creative mindset. Anyone who has heard of or believes in the laws of attraction knows what I mean and those who don't should grab a book about it and read it.

It takes getting out of the competitive mind and flowing into the creative mind to realize that what you want matters as much as what someone else wants. Being in gratitude will help you focus on the best things in life and becoming the best person you can be as well as wanting to receive only the best.

"What I want for myself I want for everyone."
-Samuel "Golden Rule Jones" Milton

Envy comes from people's ignorance of, or lack of beliefs in,

their own gifts. – Jean Vanier

CHAPTER THREE

Do You Really Want What They Have?

When I think about the art of working for yourself, I can't help but think about how we think about others, how they live and what they do for work and how much money they make. We can't help ourselves but to go there. Most of the time we imagine that those who we think make lots of money and have infinite time on their hands are some sort of "Chupacabra" (a mythical cryptic creature like "Bigfoot" that is said to inhabit parts of Latin America attacking sucking the blood from small farm animals and pets,) and their life is somehow better than ours.

Upon closer inspection, you may find that most of our lives are just as chaotic as the person who sits next to us in the next cubicle or lives in our cul-de-sac. No one man or woman is having carte blanche on time, money or mental stability.

Why is this even relevant? Why do you compare yourself to someone else? Oh, and a final question, do you really want their life? If so, why don't you want to live the one you have? I know I went really "Deepak Chopra" on you, but let's think about this.

Are you really in competition for the same dollars, same life or same job? When you purchased your car did you get the exact same one as your neighbor or something similar with the specifications you wanted to have? The company you work for pays you and also pays the person next to you. Maybe not the same salary, but close. Okay, maybe more. Just joking. But you catch my drift.

Why not take competition out of the equation and think about your work and how you live in a way that inspires you? Think of it in this way. Both you and your neighbor can have the same opportunity and both of you will look at taking advantage of this opportunity in your own way, in your own time and possibly even using different resources. The art of working for yourself begins to show itself in just this way. Do things in the way you want to do them. This is probably one the hardest things to do and re-learn. Because, doing things you want to do and in the way you want to do them takes effort. A lot of effort, until you get the hang of it. Why? Because you will encounter resistance from others.

"Do not overrate what you have received, nor envy others. He who envies others does not obtain peace of mind."

-Buddha

Where we most often slip into competition with others is when we have settled for less at some time or another in our lives. We feel we must take from others or beat them to the prize in an effort to level the playing field—be it by force, mentally or physically. Then there is the satisfaction of false justice you feel believing in part that everything is right with the universe-- culminating in some sort of an end-zone dance or happy hour with friends to brag about your conquest and how you took names and kicked butt. You weren't even thinking for a minute that what you have is not really yours were you? You didn't create it, you probably didn't even think about it until you saw it in their hands and then thought about wanting it. And, I'm sure there are some commandments, covenants or laws of attraction that have been slightly altered to justify the end results. All of which aren't good. My father always told me to run my own race. I learned this lesson well after losing my first race as a young track and field prodigy in the third grade. I was devastated when I didn't come in first place after winning every race I had run all season. My father simply gave me a big hug and asked me, "Do you think I sell a policy to everyone I meet." Not knowing any better I answered "yes." He shook his head and said, "I wish I did." He then asked me if I had tried my best. I answered, "Yes." He responded, "Then you ran your best race today. Sometimes someone else's best is better than yours and sometimes your best is better than everyone else's. All you can do is run "your" race and be the best person you can be on that day."

The man or woman who has mastered his or her mind to get whatever it is they want--without violating the rights of another--has mastered the art of working for themselves. The whole competition thing is weak and boring anyway. So is doing things by conventional means and following the herd. Yeah sure, you may consider yourself a cog in the wheel of life, but you are also an individual with independent thoughts and ideas.

Who says you can't work within a company or life's system creating your world within a world until you no longer fit? At which point you must go on and perhaps out on your own and do greater things.

It's not really your fault. We learn to compete with each other from the time we are very young. We learn to want what isn't rightfully ours through hard work towards something that we think we want but haven't dreamt about. Our modern language fully reinforces this belief. We say things like..."I Crushed Them" and "I Want to Dominate The Competition." Who are we competing against really? Sometimes, it's our own image of who we think "they" are. We have worked for someone else for so long we haven't had an independent thought since we played with G.I. Joe or Barbie. Some of us have had our spirits so deflated we suffer from an inferiority complex and even feel we lack the knowledge or education needed to work for ourselves or be successful.

When we got our jobs and started working for the man or woman was it the job we always wanted or just a place holder until we found the job we really wanted? And then we woke up and realized that we had eaten lunch with the same people for the last 15 years? Some of us even attended company picnics and workshops to improve our productivity and learn how to do more with less. Let me re-translate this. It's all about how they "the company" can get more from you.

Listen, there is absolutely nothing wrong with this kind of mentality or existence—unless it's not for you. This is how business works. If my business isn't efficient, I'm wasting money. The same goes for the company you work for. If you aren't putting out, they are wasting money. It's gotten so that most companies seem like a cross between the movies "Office Space" and "Gattaca"; we just get to wear khakis, jeans or sweat pants and they give us free bottled water and juice, that's all.

"Beware the barrenness of a busy life." - Socrates

Some of us dream of lives that are truly incredible. Actually, most of us do—but how many admit it. However, we fail to make the connection that our actions must follow our inspired thoughts. This is the rock on which most of our dreams get smashed.

We fail to put our dreams into action. Sure we sometimes make a halfhearted effort only to give up at the first sign of adversity or criticism. I too learned that to live the art of working for yourself is to take the vision of what you want and keep it firmly fixed in your mind; until you have what you want. From this mindset, you will begin to design plans to make it so. Your actions will become inspired and one with your thoughts, bringing you closer to the art of working for yourself.

This will not be easy. Most of us find it a challenge, because we have this weak and cloudy idea of what we want. We haven't taken the time to form a clear and precise thought of what it is we truly desire. You can't just have a desire to have lots of money, time on your hands and to be world traveler. Isn't that what we all want? You must create a plan, be decisive and act.

Some would argue that most of us are lazy. I would say, not really. We're just out of shape. We just haven't flexed this muscle in a long time. Think of it this way, if I were to tell you to make a phone call to your favorite pizza restaurant, you would pick up the phone and dial a particular number. You'd probably know what you want to eat because you've memorized the menu after eating there every other week since the placed showed up in your neighborhood five years ago. I bet you cannot only smell, but even taste that first bite of pizza as you are placing the order. This is the type of clarity and vision you embrace in the art of working for yourself. Creating that focused thought that is undeniably yours and yours alone.

The more we take successful action towards the life and work of our choosing the more we are living the art of working for yourself. The point I want to make is that we ultimately rise to the occasion or remain where we are due to conditions we can control if we chose to control them. When was the last time you allowed yourself to act on an inspired thought? How did it turn out?

<u>Key Observations and Obstacles</u>

As you begin to think and act in a different way, be prepared for others to notice a difference in you. Say nothing of your intentions as they may feel offended that you have not included them in your plans and may attempt to lure you back into their lives by baiting you into competition with others or themselves. They may even get angry with you and shun you. Remember, the changes you are making are about you not them.

When you begin to focus on what you want and how you are going to make it happen, it will do you good to also begin to break the habit of apologizing for what you want. Every time we speak about our actions we feel we must defend them in an effort to make others feel okay with "our" decision to do something. It's sad but true. Search your feelings the next time you find yourself in this situation. You'll find the more you talk, sometimes the more questions they have, forcing you to elaborate more, sometimes making you even question the idea in the first place, thinking "it was a crazy idea anyway."

Sometimes it's better to only share ideas and dreams in safe company--or not at all until you are ready to act.

"There are only two mistakes one can make along the road to truth: not going all the way, and not starting." - Buddha

CHAPTER FOUR

Our Best Laid Plans

When one actually thinks about planning their life I think their eyes role back in their head. I know mine used to. Then I started thinking about something. We are so engrossed in everyone else's lives, but what about our own. Which is probably why we are hooked on Reality TV, or recounting the intimate details of what your neighbor in the cubicle next to you did on their vacation and who said what to whom in the lunch room. To truly embrace the art of working for yourself you have to have a plan for your life. I don't care how intelligent you think you are, you need a practical and workable plan. You must also dream and I mean big. It's not something you can do half way. Most of us have this vague idea of the things we want to do some day. We say things like "I can't wait to retire."

Well, what the heck are you going to do then? Most of us just can't wait to not have to show up at the same place we've dreaded working at for the last 15 years, we haven't even thought beyond our last day. As my grandmother used to say "if you plan something half way, you only get half." If you know there is something you want to do in your heart, why not go for it. And I mean all of the way. I think that's why I love it when I hear people talking about going back to school to learn a new trade, get another degree, a certificate or start a business.

Usually, this is something they have thought about for a while, or that dream they wouldn't let go of.

The truth is, it's all in the planning for what we want that our life comes alive. Usually, we've planned for this thing that we are doing to really mean something in our life. This is where I often see that light beginning to shine. We are embracing the art of working for ourselves, creating a path toward living life of our terms.

The point is, stop waiting for some else's version of what you think you should do.

"A fool with a plan can outsmart a genius with no plan."
- T. Boone Pickens

For as long as I can remember I was told to get a job. That was my fate. Grow up, go to school and get a job. Be that good little worker bee. I think practically every day I heard this in some shape or form. My grandfather would say, you know, one day when you get a job, you'll see what I mean. Or my mother would look at my grades and say you're going to have to do better if you want to get a "good" job when you graduate. And let's not forget all of the job fairs I attended my junior and senior years in college.

I believe the education system we have in this country is one of the best and yet blind spot that it creates in our lives is evident. It teaches us to work for someone else. We have also been taught to deny our every desire and to work until we can't work anymore and retire.

If you love what you do does it make sense to retire? Six months after my mother passed away I called my father just to shoot the breeze and make sure he was okay. He had sold his insurance agency after my mother passed and I knew he missed her a lot. He had just walked in the house from fishing all day, which is something they used to do together quite a bit. After going over the day's fish count and stories of the ones that got away he said, "I'm going back to work, I'm tired of fishing every day and I miss insurance." You see my father loved the insurance industry so much he retired from it twice (and he knew it like the back of his hand). The first time, he sold his agency after running it for 25 years and the second time, he worked for a national carrier as a commercial underwriter and 15 years later he retired again. At that time I couldn't imagine anyone would want to come out of retirement to go back to work.

Everybody I knew back then worked for someone else or for some other reason than their own basic needs for food and shelter. From my parents to my aunts, uncles and family friends, that's the hand most of them were dealt. There was no other option. Besides, if they did it right along the way they got promoted and left the shop floor to supervise the rest of us who were left behind.

That was the real prize. To no longer do what they hired you to do. Then if the company really liked you and you stayed long enough you got a gold watch. Oh, and don't forget your pension. You're now set for life. It didn't seem like I had any control over my destiny.

My father worked as long as he wanted to work, which is part of the core of working for yourself. Why would you retire if you enjoyed what you were doing? You wouldn't, until you recognized you wanted to do something else.

For years I worked at building my agency while I also dreamed about doing something different. I think in every job I had, I did this. I was after the pay check and I was never satisfied with what I had. And that is where this journey began for me: I had to figure out why we for some reason check out for most of life as we work?

We don't necessarily hate what we do, but don't love it either. At least most of us don't. We just turn into the worker bees working and creating the nectar for the hive. Why don't we work for ourselves sooner?

"In the absence of clearly-defined goals, we become strangely loyal to performing daily trivia until ultimately we become enslaved by it." - Robert Heinlein

No wonder we ended up here. We have been told that we will be taken care of by the companies we work for, by our government and the unions we support. We are told not to worry and that they have our best interest at heart. But, where does responsibility for our own lives enter into the equation. I think right here would be as good a place as any. Here's why.

Companies owe you nothing. You though, owe it to yourself to live your best life and to get what you want. Once you do this you are starting to embrace the art of working for yourself. You are opening your mind to the possibilities of making a definite plan for your life.

They've done studies on people who have written out a plan for their lives, some in great detail. The most fascinating thing about this study is that most of the people who wrote something down accomplished just about everything they wrote down and set out to do. I believe there is magic in the writing down of what you want. Whether you keep a journal or put it on post-it notes, it is something that comes from you, created by your hands on to paper for you to see immediately. It's your energy, your words, your dreams, your life, alive and in living color or blue or black ink; depending on what you are writing with.

Most people live on the path that's been set for them (directly or indirectly); too afraid to explore their natural inclinations. But, occasionally some of us knock down all of the obstacles put in our way and take the path of our choice. The art for working for yourself is a gift you'll never know how to use--until you fight for it. My hope is that maybe one day you will create your own path. It's time you begin to re-think your life and your work. We have become too dependent on forces outside of ourselves and beyond our control, hoping and praying for a better outcome. There are times when the effort and responsibility falls squarely in our own hands and we must act.

I have watched people resist the change that is happening all around them and fight to keep things the same in an effort to not have to think or act for themselves.

"Let him who would enjoy a great future waste none of his present." - Roger Babson

Most of us don't think or act for ourselves and probably fear the thought of taking stock of the resources around us. We shy from planning for a new way of life when things are different. And for most of us change only comes when we are pushed off that rock and into the deep blue ocean of possibilities and only then do we attempt to figure out what to do and where to go next. The sad reality is, most of us swim right back to that same rock and cling to it for dear life, and stay there forever.

Change is scary, but so is not knowing what you are going to do next. This is where embracing the art of working for yourself and creating a path toward what you want and how you want to live can make change and the way you look at it more palatable, thus tempering our fear of the unknown. This is what having a plan and writing it down can do for you. It gives voice to your vision and purpose to your actions. Give it a try. Write down a few plans and see what happens. You'll be amazed at what comes next.

Key Observations and Obstacles:

So what is the next step? Getting organized is a great place to start. Clear out all of the useless clutter in your life. What are those things you've said "yes" to that you regret? Don't act like you don't know what I mean, because you roll your eyes every time you have to do whatever "it" is. Whether it is mowing the lawn or waking up at 5:30 and going to work at a job you'd rather not. No, I'm not telling you to quit your job tomorrow. But, the first step might be to look for one you enjoy that makes you the same amount of money that's 5 minutes from your home. So you can wake up 25 minutes before you have to be there and brush your teeth on the way to the office. Heck, you might even make enough to hire some else to cut your grass for you. Imagine that.

The point I want to make, is to create a plan of action that moves you one step close to the life you want. Whether you write it down or just begin to think about it.

I believe in the "Rule of 3." Simply put, do three things a day that will get you closer to your goal. Three is easy.

I started using the "Rule of 3" when I was thinking of starting my insurance agency 15 years ago. I had written out an incredibly long list of things I had to do in order to get my agency off the ground. The list looked practically insurmountable. Just as panic was setting in, I thought "well if I do three things a day I should be able to get this list under control enough to make it somewhat do-able." A funny thing happened; as I kept doing three things each day, I created a rhythm for myself. I was able to focus better on just the things I wanted and needed to do in front of me and left the rest of my list alone. All I had to do each day was cross off three things and I was done and could focus on other stuff. Three became easy. In less than a year, in the agency training program, I was ready to launch with good systems in place and a bigger book of business than I expected to have.

If you happen to have a loftier goal then you may need to get specialized training, or attend workshops and possibly go to night school. Whatever you have to do, do it. This brings you close to the art of working for yourself.

And last but not least. Plan all the way to the end! By now I'm sure you have envisioned what you want your life to look like and how it will feel when you get there. This is looking at the end result. When writing a business plan it is always recommended you begin with the end in mind. I think this is where one begins to understand the art of working for yourself. At this moment it begins to take form. Start with the vision of your life once you arrive at your destination and work backwards. Imagine how you got there and watch your plan magically come together.

"Change will not come if we wait for some other person or some other time. We are the ones we've been waiting for. We are the change we seek." – Barack Obama

CHAPTER FIVE

Lights Camera...Wait!

Since most of us work or have worked for someone else or a business for most of our adult lives, we have had most of our choices made for us--From what time we start working, to the time we retire. Yeah sure, there are some lucky ones out there that if they screamed loud enough they got their own way, got to do exactly what they wanted to do as well as how they wanted to do it. Metaphorically, these people pay the price for this. They may have been labeled selfish, self-centered and arrogant at times and perhaps some people go over the top with all of this, but if you really think about it--some of those people have the life they've always dreamed of and they've always wanted. We hate them don't we? We call them names and wish the worst for them. As if they have done you wrong personally.

The truth is that you get what you want by taking action and working and living for yourself. You cannot act nor do things where you are not. You can only act and do things from where you are, which is in your present life and in the here and now. There is also something that perplexes me to no end. Sometimes we get all of the right signals that the time is right to act and we do nothing; almost in disbelief that we are getting what we want. Why? Because, we've been told to wait. Lights (get ready), Camera (here it is), Wait (until someone else says it's okay).

You are going to let the girl or guy of your dreams walk right out of the supermarket? You've seen him or her every day for a year. She or he has smiled at you, you've smiled back and then the day comes. You reach for the same tomato. Now, you've dreamed of this day and what you were going to say and here it is. Action! It's funny to me because I used wonder how some people end up together, or how some people seemingly are so lucky. Quite simply, they take action. They know what they want and act upon it. It's just that simple.

Most people miss opportunities because they are easily influenced by the opinions of others. We then wonder why we have no desire of our own. We've stunted our ability to think for ourselves. The art of working for yourself is based in taking action. All of those plans, hopes and dreams need action to come to life.

'If you risk nothing, then you risk everything." - Geena Davis

So let's talk about work for a minute and working for someone else (or even for yourself). Why is it that when we have an idea or thought that says "do this", we're told or we tell ourselves to wait until the time is right? Some of us even automatically say, "I'll do that when I retire." Meanwhile we sit at a desk or on the couch to suffer in silence hoping to earn the right to have what we want. Why work at a job that isn't even close to what you would have chosen for yourself or run your business in a way that keeps a slave to your suppliers, customers and your fears?

What is all this waiting stuff about? What exactly are you really waiting for? I'll let you in on a little secret; there is no such thing as the perfect time for anything. Ask anyone with children. Most of us spend our entire lives waiting for that right moment for the planets to line up, for the right girl or guy to come along, or the perfect job opportunity to materialize. This is where taking action meets reality. This is where the art of working for yourself comes to life. Acting on those ideas and dreams will bring you the life you've always wanted.

They say that most of us are perfect starters but horrible finishers. Well, some of us don't even make it out of the gate, paralyzed by fear and procrastination. Two of the worst enemies of our dreams. In order to really understand the art of working for yourself you must eliminate fear and procrastination from your life. They will kill all of your dreams and stop you dead in your tracks, making action impossible. We tell ourselves that there is always something that is going to happen, or "if" I do this, "then" I can't do that. As my dad always said "If, if and buts, were candy and nuts, everyday would be Christmas." Lose the "if" and "buts" and take action. Follow that plan you have for that dream vacation you've always wanted to take or start that business around that idea you've had for the last twelve years.

No time like the present. The funny thing is that most of our fears turn out to be the monster under the bed. Something that we've made up that is never there.

"Twenty years from now you will be more disappointed by the things that you didn't do than by the ones you did do. So throw off the bowlines. Sail away from the safe harbor. Catch the trade winds in your sails. Explore. Dream. Discover. "

- Mark Twain

There is something that happens when we start moving towards what we want. It's called "life." It's like finding that perfect someone or asking for something and getting it exactly how you want it. You know it right away. Your heart tells you immediately, because your whole energy changes. You begin to act in a way that is truer to who you really are. I like to say, you start to believe in yourself. Taking action puts you in the driver seat of your life.

So it's "Moving Day." It was a March 2nd, 1993 and I had already decided that I was moving to Seattle, Washington. My sister asked me if I would wait until the weekend to leave and I told her that I thought and felt I should leave the next day. A snow storm was coming and I felt if I stayed it would trap me there for longer than three more days. She said, " Fine. You can leave but you must promise me that you will stop in a major city every night and call me when you get off of the road and let me know you are okay. Oh and I have to leave before you do because I don't want you to see me cry. I hate good-bye's." I began my journey on March 3rd driving the whole day through, and as I got off of the road that evening I realized it was snowing a little and just knew I'd be facing a winter storm in the morning. So I called my sister and turned in for the night. The next day when I awoke I turned on the TV to check the weather ahead, only to find out that Ohio and the rest of the East Coast was under a blanket of snow and magically there was but a trace on the ground where I was. The sun started to shine and stayed that way all the way to Seattle. As I think about the actions of my life, I now know that there must be meaning in my actions. There should be some reason why I do something and how I do it. What is the end result I expect to see?

Waiting always comes with a price. I am so glad I didn't wait to leave, for had I waited, would I have left or would I have continued to delay? How often have you done something like this yourself? Why not trust your gut when it speaks to you?

It doesn't matter if you are working for a Fortune 500 company or own the corner store, the art of working for yourself mindset will begin to take shape when you take action. There is no textbook something or a checklist of sorts to work through and then you are magically thinking and working for yourself.

It's a way of being that will begin to transcend everything you do. In the next chapter I'll talk more about this mindset thing.

Key Observations and Obstacles

Being decisive will make or break you. You see most of us aren't decisive at all. I'll even add myself to the list. It's taken me a while to get here. But having your mind firmly fixed on what it is you desire and committing to take action is the foundation of the art of working for yourself. Nothing starts without the thought and the thought never materializes unless you take action, deliberate action.

So stop procrastinating and do it! The more successful actions you take the easier it becomes to take another action and another and another. Then the momentum of great things happening for you and to you will manifest itself in your life and the art of working for yourself will be yours.

Always remember to keep the spirit of persistence in your heart. For there will be times when you run into obstacles that will test your resolve. This is where the universe will test you to see how badly you really want to do what it is you set out to do. Make persistence your ally and it will light your path towards your goal.

"Happiness is when what you think, what you say and what you
do are in harmony – Mahatma Gandhi

CHAPTER SIX

Getting You Out Of Your Head

It's been said that if someone were to say the things to us that we say to ourselves --we'd punch them in the mouth. I know this is true, because I've said some pretty messed up things to myself. Hardly supportive of my dreams and goals. Things that make me really shake my head, either trying to motivate myself or punish myself for failing at something, and some are even echoes of the words of others. Have you ever listened to yourself? Really listened to yourself?

No, not that stuff you think in your head trying to be clever before giving a toast or when you're mad at the driver that just cut you off. I mean the things you tell yourself when you wake-up in the morning before you set your feet on the floor. What do you think when the alarm clock goes off? Is it some form of "I hate my job", I can't stand…", "I wish…?" The mind is a very powerful thing and our un-conscious mind is even more so.

The art of working for yourself requires you to change your thinking. Begin to think of yourself as worthy of living and being and doing what you've always imagined. Begin talking and thinking in a way that honors your vision of who you are. The job you have right now may not be you or where you want to be. You must begin to think of it terms of a stepping stone or the launch pad for where you want to go. The same goes for entrepreneurs and business owners. A seed never stays a seed once it has been planted in the ground and given the water of life and fertile soil to sink its roots into. It grows into a great big tree or a beautiful flower.

What you tell yourself matters. If you begin your day in negativity, that's the direction you will most likely follow for that day and the days after until you decide to think in a different way. With starts like this, how will you ever reach the point where you are doing your best work?

It took me a while to get this. I was always coming from a place of negativity (masked as passive- aggression, of course, with a slight smile so you could never tell how disappointed or sad I was.) It was always someone else's fault or one incredible excuse after another on why I never got what I wanted or expected that made every day doomsday. Believe it or not, what you tell yourself affects your beliefs, your attitude and even your actions and your results.

Athletes are coached to visualize the actions they need to take to be victorious. That's exactly what you should do with your life. When I think of visualizing I often go back to the 1980 NBA Finals between L.A. Lakers vs. Philadelphia 76'ers. I watched a man known as Julius "Dr. J" Erving defy gravity by doing a move that is now simply called "The Up and Under" (watch it on YouTube, it's incredible.) As Dr. J was going to the hoop he was about to be forced out of bounds or he would have to take jump shot. But instead, he took off from one side of the basket and going up and under the backboard and laid it up on the glass on the other side of the backboard, practically floating out of bounds and back in bounds to make the basket. At 16, watching this live on TV, it blew my mind. I couldn't imagine how he did this. In time, I realized that it all started with his thoughts. While he may not have visualized that move in just that way, he knew he had to make the basket or go out of bounds and the other team would get the ball.

Visualizing brings your thoughts and your body into harmony. I do this LAST THING at night as I drift off to sleep and FIRST THING when I awake in the morning. As I drift off to sleep I think about my day and wonder how I can make tomorrow better and when I awake I visualize how I want my day to look. It doesn't usually take long. Usually, about ten to fifteen minutes. I visualize a brief list of actions that I've taken or want to take that will bring me closer to my goal. In working for yourself, visualization is a great way to design the outline of the plan you have for yourself--in great detail.

Usually, when we are visualizing we see things exactly as we want them to be. I've heard some call it daydreaming and fantasizing. People say it like it's a bad thing. We often stop our daydreams before they leave our minds, because we've been taught to believe that having a daydream is useless and a waste of time.

I believe it is necessary for you to foster your dreams. I say daydream as often as you can. You need to imagine it before you can build it. Remember that.

"Do what you can, where you are, with what you have."

- Theodore Roosevelt

We've also been taught to believe that life is hard and what you want is wrong. How dare you ask for what you want? That's just greedy. Who do you think you are? Oh, it doesn't stop there. That may have been when you are a kid. It gets even worse when you are an adult. If those words are so deep in your head, they are now on an incessant loop like the evening news. I'll just stop there because you'd want to stop reading and I want to you read further. No need to call Dr. Phil.

Here's the deal. Remember when you were a kid and you pretended you were an astronaut who built a spaceship that had bananas for fuel? What happened to that girl who dreamed of being a ballerina in the Nutcracker? Or the little boy who wanted to be the veterinarian for aliens. The point I'm making is that there was a time when you believed everything was possible, and nothing was impossible. You didn't know there were any rules to break. You made your own rules. You even changed them whenever you felt like it: Even if your brother got mad at you.

That's the mindset you have to develop to embrace the art of working for yourself. There are no rules and what you want and how you want it matters. Especially, when it comes to how you work and live. I know you probably work for someone else right now physically and mentally. That's okay for now. You are learning a new way of life and it may take a minute to move your thinking in a new direction. You are actually re-learning a way to think.

A colleague of mine, John Erdman once told me, "That when we live outside our core values and needs, our life takes on a view of something other than our own. Our personality becomes something other than who we are. This causes us to do and act in ways that aren't true to our thoughts and vision of how we dream of living and doing."

So what does this look like? We punish ourselves and those around us by treating ourselves and others horribly. We go through the motions of work and life, hoping someone will see our pain and have mercy on us and set us free by magically approving of everything we do. We pray we win the lottery or some other such wackiness as though winning a lot of money is the answer to our problems. It's not. Even with a healthy bank account, we ultimately aren't working for ourselves if we don't have the best mindset.

"In life we do things Some we wish we had never done. Some we wish we could replay a million times in our heads. But they all make us who we are. And in the end they shape every detail about us. If we were to reverse any of them we wouldn't be the

person we are. So just live. Make mistakes. Have wonderful memories. But never ever second guess who you are, where you have been. And most importantly where it is you're going."

- Anonymous

As you begin to embrace this "art form" you will surround yourself with people who are already on this path or at least moving in the direction you want to go. You must also stay away from the doomsday crowd. In an effort to be liked, we sometimes surround ourselves with the wrong people our whole lives. These are people who aren't going anywhere and probably bumbling on the same path we're on or those who basically destroy almost every single chance we have at creating something remarkable by laughing at what we do or planting seeds of doubt in our heart and minds and in some extreme cases even mentally or physically beating it out of us. It's no wonder that some of us have ended up where we are. You know the ones.

They say birds of a feather flock together. Well, they usually all sit together at the same lunch table too. They know every reason in the book why things won't work as well as every conspiracy theory there is. Conversely, what is equally contagious is associating with people who are working for themselves and are moving in a positive direction in their lives.

As my father used to tell me while fishing on Lake Erie, "a high tide raises all boats." And we had a little boat. So put your boat in the water and let the tide raise it to where it's supposed to be. You'll never find new horizons anchored in the harbor.

Key Observations and Obstacles

I believe we all have intuition or psychic ability within us— which we can cultivate once we acknowledge it. We sometimes instinctually know when it is time to do something or leave a situation. Most of the time we usually dismiss it and allow that pivotal moment to pass. In these moments, we are missing sometimes a powerful opportunity to be and do more.

It's also been said that within our creativity lies a sixth sense. Within our imaginations the possibilities are endless and we can do anything. I would also argue that the art of working for yourself comes from your ability to embrace your intuition and know what it is you need to do--in order to find the path of your best life. The laws of nature are at work everywhere all the time and there are times when they defy logic and things happen that seem impossible: Making the art of working for yourself possible.

"Your vision only becomes clear when you can look into your own heart. One who looks outside, dreams: One who looks inside, awakes." – Carl Jung

CHAPTER SEVEN

Hidden In Plain Sight

I was watching "The Karate Kid" (2010 version) not too long ago when Mr. Han said something to his young apprentice named Dre' that stunned me. I would like to share it with you because I think many of us need to be reminded and OFTEN of this observation. He said "Your focus needs more focus" to young Dre' as he was attempting to learn the art of Kung Fu.

I think of the many times when I thought I was focusing on my life--when in reality I was not. I spent so much time worried about what everyone else was doing and what they thought. Heck, I didn't even zoom in. So what is this all about really? My knee-jerk reaction is that we don't care what we do or where we work. But we really do, or else we wouldn't get angry when things don't turn out right and the way we want them to. We dream about it, even pray about it, and yet somehow we often fall short of our wants and dreams.

So what happens? Dulled by the unfulfilled dreams we've since let go of in the name of making a living, our focus gets a little blurry. I remember when I worked as a customer service representative at an insurance company for almost five years before discovering that I could have joined the company's agency training program--which would put me on the track to having my own business that much sooner. Instead, I got sucked in by the perfect schedule (11am to 8pm). You didn't have to tell me twice. I could get up late and go to bed late. Meanwhile, I was wishing I had my own business never realizing it was right under my nose. So there I was, not zooming in for almost 5 years. They say what you focus on you hit. You never hear of a sniper aiming at the sky hoping to hit the target. Yet, when most of us finished school that's what we did. Sure we interviewed at a few places and then we sold out to the highest bidder offering stock options and the ability to wear jeans, drink all the bottled water and cold juice from the fridge whenever we wanted. Some of us took the job making the most money.

Listen, I'll be the first to say it. I like money and I did the same thing. Did I really stop to think what the heck I was doing or looked at the company and understood what I'd be signing on for? No! I'm not saying you need to hire a forensic accountant to give you a report on the future of the company you go to work for.

It's much plainer than that. Do you like what you will be doing? Is this going match the goals you have planned for yourself? Did you plan goals for yourself and does the offer match up enough with the goals? These are the questions that give us focus and direction to embrace exactly what we want. The only way to get focused is to determine what you want, honor what you want and create a direct path toward it.

Consider this. That venus fly trap of a job offer is the vaseline on the lens of life. We seem to slowly drift left of center, far away from what we really want when it is placed before us. It sometimes gets snapped back into clear view when we get passed over for that corner office; that was in a weird way given to the Jake the brown-noser that sits behind you. The ugly truth of this is that Jake knew what he wanted and went for it. So don't be mad. This is exactly what I'm talking about. Focus is something that takes discipline and steady, constant practice to do consistently well.

"The greatest danger for most of us is not that our aim is too high and we miss it, but that it is too low and we reach it."
- Michelangelo

Are you in the habit of chasing the shiny bobble? That next latest and greatest thing, or doing all of things everyone says you are supposed to do to live you best life. When you dance from lily pad to lily pad you are robbing yourself of direction. Always chasing and grasping for the energy of that fleeting thing that you think you want most. A lot of time if you just stand still and practice being "present" and focus, the art of working for yourself will reveal itself to you. I can't tell you how many times I emptied my bank account to buy the coolest thing going, all the while supposedly saving for a new car or something equally important. Only to curse the universe when the car I was currently driving broke down. It is in our focus that we take note of all that is around us, thus finding our clarity and purpose.

When I think back to when I worked for someone other than myself and even working for myself. I remember awakening to the fact that to the trained eye, there is so much happening around us; it will simply astound you. Things rarely change overnight. Companies don't just up and move to a new city or go out of business without warning signs (typically). It's a gradual thing. Perks disappear, they change the bonus structure, departments vanish and people get offered early retirement. I am not saying these are always the signs, but when you understand the art of working for yourself you begin to focus on you and the direction that feels right to your soul.

If you own a business, markets change, suppliers stop calling, your employee quits, your spouse leaves you. These could all be signs that you are not focusing on you, your business (if you love it) or your focus needs a little more focus. Believe me, I know. I am a business owner and a few of these things have happened to me and it sharpened my focus immediately. Talk about gaining clarity. So when things don't exactly set right with you, stop and take inventory from that place of awareness deep inside you and decide what your next step is. You decide, not someone else. Hey, I get it sometimes it's best to let some things go and or change your focus. But again, knowing when to even do this is understanding the art of working for yourself.

Focus takes effort. It takes persistence. This is an essential factor in creating the life you've always wanted for yourself. It is through your focus that this can be accomplished. Most people who know the art of working for themselves are sometimes misunderstood. Again some people call them bullet-proof employees or the "non-stick" entrepreneurs. They are often disguised as a slacker, or someone who comes in on time and leaves on time, someone whose businesses always seem to work out, a brown-noser and even the kid whose mother got him the job.

What we fail to realize is that these people have the basic roots of one who works for themselves. They are focused on their lives and how it fits with whom they see themselves as, not your life and definitely not the companies they work for. They are not their job or business. They are themselves all the time or at least most of it.

"Most people have no idea of the giant capacity we can immediately command when we focus all of our resources on mastering a single area of our lives."
- Anthony Robbins

Now, I am sure that you are reading this book for a reason and unless you are one of the many with a definite goal in life and know how you are going to make it happen, most might read this and let it fly over their head. The starting point for one's desire is focus. Most of us are pretty good at starting things and horrible at finishing them. Whatever reason you have for reading this book, now is the time to create a new habit and focus on what it is you want, how you want it and what you plan to give in return for it.

Focus is what turns that little orange flame into a white hot torch of expectation, melting every doubt in its path. In the next chapter I want to talk you about faith and how the art of working for yourself makes you stronger mentally and emotionally.

Key Observations and Obstacles:

Beyond your focus you must use your will to make things move in the direction you want them to go. So how do you use your willpower effectively? Often, when we think of willpower we think of saying "no" to that third jelly doughnut, or in my case that next glass of wine. We seldom make use of the will for a positive thing. Okay, maybe in sports and even then we think of it as a force we access to beat someone. Well, here is where I challenge you to get personal and think of your willpower and ask yourself how do you plan to use it. First, you are creating something..."Your Life", and second this has nothing to do with anyone else except you. Even if you have a family or caring for a dying relative. Your will comes from you and is all you and about you and what you want to create and allow into your life.

It all begins with you. If you are not strong then nothing you touch will be either. It's like building a house on a weak foundation. It will eventually fall down. Your will allows you the strength and tenacity to build something great. Also, remember the proper use of the will is to never to use it at the expense of another. Your will is that undeniable light that says I can do this. I will do this.

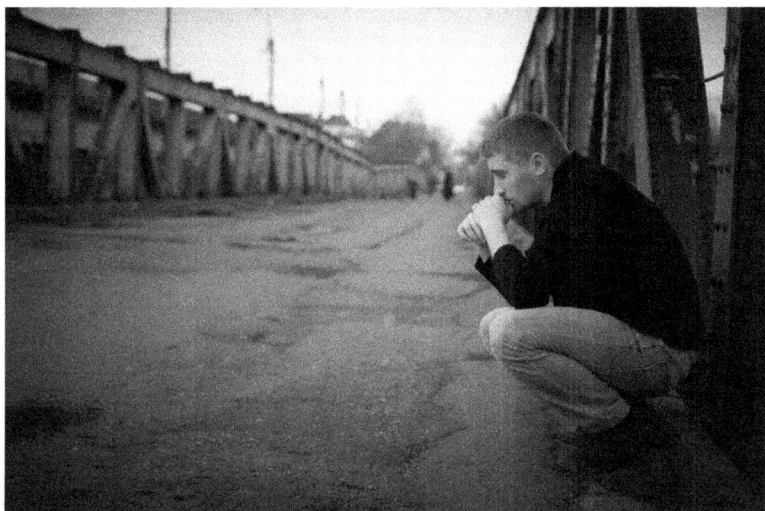

"It's the repetition of affirmations that leads to belief. And once that belief becomes a deep conviction, things begin to happen."

– Muhammad Ali

CHAPTER EIGHT

You Just Gotta Believe

They say that faith, love and sex are some of the most powerful of our major emotions. But, just so we don't go down the wrong road, I think we should leave love and sex out of the conversation for the time being. I'm sure based on how the last chapter ended you're probably thinking I might break into some form of God talk and how we can be more like Jesus, Buddha, Mother Teresa and Confucius.

The truth is no matter what you believe, your faith is the foundation on which the art of working for yourself begins. Faith takes your focus, your energy, your plans and mixes them with your own thoughts and turns them into reality. They say faith has more to do with the subconscious mind or the unconscious mind than one's conscious mind and I believe that to be true. Proof of this can be found in how one prays for or asks for something. It's all in the way you pursue it. You have to go after it as if you are going to get it. When you ask in this way the probability of it appearing or you attaining the goal is pretty close to 100% or let's say at least 90%. I'm not kidding.

When I think back to when I split from my business partner to go it alone in the insurance industry, all I had was my belief that it was going to happen, just the way I always dreamed and planned it would. I had my business plan that I had written and rewritten six times and friends and family wishing me well. In the end things turned out better than I ever could have imagined. What I planned for paled in comparison to what actually showed up. It was incredible. We've all been told at one time or another, you just gotta believe. Well this is belief in action.

Think of your children, nieces and nephews or that kid in the checkout line you'd love to taze because he or she won't stop doing their annoying end-zone dance until their mother or father gives in and lets them have some chocolate, gum or something else sticky or gooey from the candy rack. Through a positive lens interpretation of that illustration; kids truly believe in the "why not" of life. Or more correctly "the why" of life. Why, gets you to the core of your beliefs in the how you are going to get to that which is true to you. I know this sounds backwards, because it's illogically correct.

"You can have anything you want if you will give up the belief that you can't have it." - Robert Anthony

Here's how it works. First, logic has nothing to do with anything. We want what we want and this outlook is how the art of working for yourself gets you out of the habit of thinking that everyone else's wants are more important than your own. It's not about being selfish, mind you. Why though, shouldn't you have a piece of life that gets you the exact amount of money you desire, doing exactly what you've always wanted to do and how you want to do it? Most of us know, there is that something we know we want and even how to get it and still we do nothing about it? Why? Society has stripped the "why and "why not's" out of most of us and here is how you get it back. When you ask someone "why they want to do something", it drives right to the heart of feeling. I used to get defensive and almost throw my back out after the hairs on the back of my neck stood up as I would go through the maze of emotions--when someone had the audacity to ask me "why I want to do something." I mean, how could they ask that question? Don't they understand that you've had this dream since grade school? Actually, they may not, so when they ask, take the opportunity to tell them with understated conviction, but don't feel the need to justify a thing.

Know that in telling them, they may not understand your motivation and why should they? It's your dream. So don't spend too much time telling them the "why." It's better to show them. Our parents always told us that actions speak louder than words." Well, this is one case where actions mean the most. This is where our actions--supported by our beliefs--create results. Imagine thinking about something so much that in your mind you have planned out every detail, shape size, color and smell. The "why" seems to take care of itself. So when anyone asks the questions of why you want to leave your job or how are you going to eat? You can tell them what you are going to do and how you are going to do it and they will believe you, because you believe in you. Then you will show them *with your actions*. That's how faith works.

Sometimes we get all mystical and other worldly when we talk about this topic. I understand it. Because, in the end having faith in our dream of living the way we want or working for yourself is huge. It's what we whom aim to work for ourselves aspire to. It's the blanket in which our dreams are wrapped, protected from others who would try and steal them from our hearts and minds.

Efforts to sideline dreams happen every day. While we watch television, listen to the radio and even go to the mall. We are told what we should believe and why. You don't believe me? Go turn on the radio for five minutes and take in the content at its most basic level. What do you hear? Then, give yourself the gift of an information blackout. Don't watch TV or use the internet for a month and see what happens. No, your life won't fall apart. However, you won't miss much and you might enjoy thinking about things you've long since forgotten.

"I am convinced all of humanity is born with more gifts than we know. Most are born geniuses and just get de-geniused rapidly."
- Buckminster Fuller

What Bucky Fuller suggests IS what happens when we go on vacation. Our mind relaxes and our dreams begin to flow back into our minds and hearts again. We start to believe it's possible to find a way to live on that island, own a coffee shop and surf all day. So much so that we spend half of the time actually trying to really do the math and figuring out how to actually buy that surfer's coffee shop on the beach. Then the Mai Tai's wear off, you're bringing your seat and trays back into the up and locked positions, again! You grab your carry-on bag and forget it ever happened--or perhaps you don't.

This is where having a plan, getting out of your own head and having a little faith come together. I'm not telling you to quit your job yet, just start thinking about the art of working for yourself and thinking of the possibilities. Now, I'm sure you can feel your heart beating a little faster and it may feel like it is about to jump out of your chest right about now. This reaction is normal. You might even have a little fear flowing through your head and heart. So I'll start there in the next chapter.

Key Observations and Obstacles

Self-Confidence is something we could all use a booster shot of every now and then, especially when we are beginning something new in life. Knowing you have the ability to do a thing is so important. It's probably as important as knowing that you have the willpower to make happen what you set your mind to. Hold the image of what you want, fixed in your mind until you attain it. Write this as a vivid vision and keep it somewhere you can look at it from time to time--as a reminder of what it is you want. I've seen some people create dream books and dream boards. I've used post it notes! By doing these simple concrete things and creating tangible references to your aspirations, your self-confidence will rise to a level you've probably never before experienced. It's wonderful what happens next when one adopts these practices. Excuses and reasons why things can't be done evaporate. You are happier and you become more self-reliant.

There will be some who think that you are lucky. Well, I don't believe there is such a thing as luck. Luck is when opportunity meets action which most of the time looks like chance allowing you to take advantage of the situation laid before you.

When you begin to become aware of the opportunities around you, it will seem as if they are all falling at your feet like manna from heaven. Then take notice and become fully aware--you are working for yourself.

"The thing you fear most has no power. Your fear of it is what has the power. Facing truth will really will set you free."

– Oprah Winfrey

CHAPTER NINE

The Scary Part

There are a couple of fears that come to mind when I talk to people about the art of working for yourself. The fear of criticism and the fear of poverty are two that jump out more often than not. I know the word poverty is such a harsh word. I'm sure there are others you can think of but these two are at the top of my list and probably yours too. If you have read this far, my hope is that you will be willing to read a little further.

The truth of the matter is there are times in our life when we are all scared of something. Whether it's the boogey man, your boss or your parents, fear is a powerful thing. But the two fears mentioned above, the fear of criticism and the fear of poverty are at the top of the list for most of us. I believe when your heart and mind is filled with fear, you are robbed of the chance to making prompt decisions. Chances are you will also share those fearful thoughts with whomever you come in contact with, possibly sending them down the same path. It wreaked havoc in my life for years. Sometimes, I think I was afraid of my own shadow. It felt as if I was going to be found out and someone would tell me I was a bad person and didn't deserve anything. Fear is contagious. It's been said that animals can smell fear. Well, so can people. We just don't recognize it as such. It's pure biology and energy. We're just on the upper end of the food chain of the animal kingdom, that's all. We are better off when we prepare to deal with the fear that will pass through us.

I bet if you were to ask any random person on the street what they fear, most would say "I fear nothing." This in most cases is untrue, because most people don't recognize that they are so beaten down mentally, emotionally and spiritually--by some type of fear--that they don't even want to think about what fears they have. Our fears have taken us over in such a subtle way. Some of us go our whole life with this weight on our backs not realizing what it is.

"To live your life in the fear of losing it is to lose the point of life." - Malcolm Forbes

Let's start with considering the fear of criticism, because I think this is where a lot of our fears begin. This fear is cultivated from a very young age when we are children. Our parents, friends, family and the neighborhood bully...bless their hearts all meant well trying to shape us into productive members of society. Receiving criticism used to crush me; especially the kind that was mean and hurtful. But I guess when you don't have a firm sense of who you are and what you want, it's all cruel. What I learned is that when you react to criticism in a defensive way it diverts you away from who you are and what you want to be. Some of the most horrendous decisions and actions I've taken in my life were all attempts to avoid criticism; I see that clearly in hindsight. Ultimately though, so much damage is done to our dreams, likes and dislikes and our sense of what is possible. It was "advice" handed out free of charge in heaping tablespoons of so-called tough love or just plain meanness. It is probably the one thing in life everyone has had too much of. In fact I'd even go so far as to call it a crime. What's planted is fear in our hearts and resentment in our minds, thus blocking any chance of attracting the things we truly want.

Consider this: As long as we're scared, where dreams are concerned, we don't think we can have them or deserve them. Is this really how you want to live out your life?

Why don't we believe in fairy tales anymore? Easy, because we fear criticism. We don't want people to think we're immature, dumb, unintelligent and probably a few other undesirable things. Heck, people have been burned at the stake in this country for less and probably still are in a few others.

Our media and society also has done a number on us by fostering the power of the fear of criticism. What percentage of the news is negative compared to positive?

Businesses actually thrive on it. They call it planned obsolescence. And many a consumer follows in lock step like mice to the "Pied Piper" having to have the next latest and greatest thing if only to feed our ego.

It becomes about keeping up with "The Smith's" so others don't think we don't have it like "that" and avoid being...criticized for not doing well or having enough. I'm sure you can think of more so, I'll stop there for now.

"If you just set out to be liked, you would be prepared to compromise on anything at any time, and you would achieve nothing." - Margaret Thatcher

So what then about the fear of poverty, which is probably hands down one of the most destructive things I can think of that limits one's ability to work for themselves? It's serious enough to crush anyone's chances of reaching any goal set. It corrupts your ability to be reasonable, your ability to dream of things greater than you currently have, kills your thoughts of independence and makes self-control next to impossible. It's no wonder we fear poverty and especially those who have experienced it first hand and earlier in life. Our early environmental experience and conditioning stays with us and ultimately we must make peace with our story of origin—which is entirely possible.

Let's face it. No one wants to be poor, or what they think poor is. I think that's why we chase money so feverishly. We fear not having it and for some will do most anything to get it. It's been said that this world is rich with more resources than we could ever need and yet those who don't have much "want" and those who have a lot "want even more." Do you ever wonder how some people appear to be incredibly lucky while others can't seem to catch a break?

The very fear of poverty itself is actually a state of mind. No more, no less. And so goes the art of working for yourself along this same road. For it is in understanding and extinguishing this fear of poverty that we can travel this road more easily, thus embracing this mindset completely.

As you move past these two major barriers to success you will dismiss all doubts, for there will be no place for them. Instead your thoughts will be grounded in the courage of possibilities and expectations of what you want from your life and how you want to live it. Those who criticize you will fade away and your fear of poverty will be replaced with abundance and a sense of direction.

"If you ever reach the point when you've had enough, would you recognize it?" – Anonymous

As for other fears you may face, they will be revealed as you take inventory of your life. Be committed to dealing with them directly on this journey. And as you take them on, they too will be replaced with a confidence and a knowing that you can handle anything that comes your way--because you are now in control of your heart and mind. With renewed energy, fill your mind with whatever you can conceive. You are in control of your own thoughts, your environment and can create the life you've always wanted because you now work for yourself.

Key Observations and Obstacles:

Having addressed our fears, it is time to lose the alibis and the reasons why we can't work for ourselves. Most of us go through life asking the question "what if this happens" or "if this happens then I'll do that." I'll never forget the day before my mother passed away. I was trying my best to catch a flight back home from Germany. She knew I was well on my way to living one of my dreams. I had always wanted to see Europe and now I was living there. We had occasionally talked about my dreams and what I wanted to do with my life when I was younger. Not realizing this was the last time I would ever speak to her, as we ended our conversation she said to me, "Never look back on your life and say "what if." I love you. Take care." These too are words that have always stuck with me.

Since then I have come to realize this was one of the most powerful and useful things ever said to me. I used to be the "King of What if." So I will end this chapter with what I feel are some of my deepest thoughts on these two words.

When I look back I would "What If" the world to death. And then I thought "What if" I would discover my true self and live my best life? Then I might have a chance to understand the mistakes I've made and learn something from the experience of others, because I know now there is nothing wrong with me. I wish had spent more time discovering my strengths and less time building alibi's to cover my weaknesses.

It's funny, I think building alibi's with which to explain away failure has become a global phenomenon. The habit is as old as time itself and it is fatal to one's success. Why do people cling to their beloved alibis? The answer is obvious. We defend our alibis because we create them! Our alibis are the fruit of our imagination. It is human nature to defend one's own mental offspring.

My habit of building alibis was deeply rooted. I always had some reason "why" I couldn't or didn't do "X", which usually involved some sort of supernatural or miraculous force that made it impossible for me to accomplish what I said I was going to do or wanted to do. I've been told habits are difficult to break, especially when they provide justification for something we do. Plato had this truth in mind when he said, "The first and best victory is to conquer self. To be conquered by self is, of all things, the most shameful and vile."

Napoleon Hill, author of "Think and Grow Rich" wrote: "Life is a checkerboard, and the player opposite you is time. If you hesitate before moving, or neglect to move promptly, your men will be wiped off the board by time. You are playing against a partner who will not tolerate indecision."

When I look back, I thought I had a logical excuse for not having forced life to come through with whatever I asked. Happily, that alibi is now obsolete, because I am in possession of the knowledge that unlocks the door to "The Art of Working for Yourself" and life's other gems.

Nothing will be held against you for using this knowledge, but there is a price you must pay if you do not use it. The price is continuing to live the life you've always lived, all the while wishing for something to be different. I can only show you the path. It is you who must walk it. There is a life of incredible opportunity that awaits if you put this knowledge to use.

It is the satisfaction that comes to all who conquer self and force life to pay whatever is asked. What are you waiting for? Don't just think you are working for yourself. Know you are!

Is this reward worthy of your effort? I hope this book will help you make the start and be convinced that "the art of working for yourself is for you." It is time you trust yourself. You've come to this fork in the road time and time again only to continue choosing the same path. You know where it leads. It's time to choose a new way of life.

My hope is that you will share this book and its ideas with others creating a collective wave of change in the way we all work and live.

Remember, no matter who you work for, always work for yourself.

"Your time is limited, so don't waste it living someone else's life. Don't be trapped by dogma – which is living the results of other people's thinking. Don't let the noise of other's opinions drown out your own inner voice. And most important, have the courage to follow your heart and intuition. They somehow already know what you truly want to become. Everything else is secondary."

– Steve Jobs

CHAPTER TEN

Well Get Busy Already!

So now that you've read this far I'm hoping that your mind is buzzing with ideas and things you'd like to do. So I've put together a few things that might help you get things started. First things first however. Don't rush into this. This will be your first reaction to this new energy. I need for you to sit with this for a minute or a day or two and think. Allow your mind to open up--and I mean wide. Think of the possibilities, all the possibilities. Remember, you are and will be making some changes that could potentially crack the planet on which you live. So this is something I urge you to take very seriously and give one hundred percent of your focus to as you begin to embrace the art of working for yourself.

<u>Number One:</u> Write out your "Dream List"

This is a list of all of the things you ever wanted to do. Even back as far as childhood and I dare you to allow yourself to go there. What I've done is used a legal pad and physically written down everything that popped into my head--no matter how ridiculous it sounded. I allowed myself to get used to allowing my thoughts of what I wanted to have or be, come to life on a page and be expressed by me. I did not edit my thoughts. Every crazy thought was fair game. Free from any judgment of my wants and desires. The funny thing that started to happen was when I would read them aloud, I would begin to try and form a plan of how I was going to accomplish some of my wild ideas. Believe me some of them were pretty darn wild and crazy. But, I began to know that the possibilities were there to make them happen. This is the fun part. Let yourself dream of things actually being and creating them.

Now, if you are like me, your list will be long. Mine was about five legal pages long. It will look overwhelming as you look at all of this paper. Just breathe a little and know you don't have to do all of this stuff. It's only a list. A list that you can begin to pick from to do what you want to do. As you go back and read it you may also start to cross some things off of it as you realize there are some things you probably don't want to do, they just sounded like a good idea at the time. I had a few of those. The point is to learn to think in an unlimited way.

Number Two: Show me the Money!

Just how much are we talking about here? Let's face it, some of us do things solely for the money. The question we should ask ourselves; is there a particular dollar amount you have in mind when you say you want a lot of money? Is it as vague as when you hear someone say I'm a millionaire? What does that actually mean? $1 Million or $999 Million? There is a big difference there. It's time to get specific.

Let's start with your bank account. How much is in there? Better yet, how much is in your wallet? That's an even more practical place to start. Why? I'll tell you why. Because, if you don't feel like you can go in a store and buy whatever you want without checking your bank balance or wondering when your credit card billing cycle rolls over, then that's what you think about when you think about how much money you have, need and want. This is your ground zero. Nowhere to go but up from here. Next, look at your expenses. Is it time to clean house? I did this not too long ago and was floored at some of the things I was paying for that had services that overlapped or I wasn't using any more. It added up to almost $400 a month (multiply that by 12...). I'm not kidding.

This isn't about being cheap. It's about being smart with your money and not wasting it.

Here's something to think about before you say yes to buying a service or gadget you don't need. A). Do I have something like this at home I don't use anymore or never used? B). Is this or will this replace something that is broken? And C). Can I combine this with something I'm already paying for that can be done cheaper? Now, there are just some things you've got to have. I know I do. So here is what I say to myself. "Self, you want this, and you won't stop thinking about it or talking about it until you get it. But, if you get it you better freakin' use it." This way I don't feel like I am throwing money away. I've also developed a 6 Month Rule to test myself and how I use things. It goes like this. You might want to try it. It works, and I mean like clockwork. "If I have not used, worn or touched (X) in a 6 month period of time I must sell it or give it away." Now, if I begin to feel guilty because I couldn't stand to part ways with that treadmill I bought two years ago, swearing I was going to train for a triathlon, then I give myself an additional six months and if I don't even breathe in that direction, it's outta here."

Believe me it works. Give it a try. You'll be amazed at how much stuff you'll let go of. The key here is to begin to look at where you spend your money and the space things take up in your life. I like to think I'm trading stuff for experiences.

Next, if you have the courage to go here. Talk about your money. This is final frontier as far as I'm concerned. It's up there with sex, religion and politics. We never talk about money. We've been taught not to ask about it, to take what we are given and to not want too much of it. It's all bad. See, you are even feeling guilty and scared while you are reading this, aren't you?

Money allows you to live and enjoy life on your terms. There is a big difference between wanting money just to have it and wanting it to use to enjoy and have the things you need in your life. We've been conditioned by media, family and friends to feel our life is worthless unless we are living the life of the rich and famous. Look back in the previous paragraphs. How much stuff do you really need? Search your heart and feel what you need. How much of it is visual noise? In the words of my father. "Why do I need to buy all of this stuff to impress a bunch of people I don't like or know."

If you are understanding the art of working for yourself like I think you are, money will only be a by-product of what you do and need to enjoy your life. It is not tied to the desperate race to compete with "The Smith's" down the block all the while checking your bank balance to make sure you can afford it. You won't be concerned with what others are doing or what they have. You simply won't.

What are your limiting beliefs about money? Who told you how much was too much? Who told you "Money is evil?" Or, "You can't afford that?" And, "You don't need this?" The list goes on and on, I'm sure. I urge you to challenge these words in your mind that stop you from making the amount of money you feel you want and deserve. If you think you are poor, then you are. If you think you are rich, then you are. It's just that simple. Being rich is relative. Do you have everything you need and want? Then you are there. You are what most people would consider "Rich."

Last but not least. Keep extreme track of your daily expenses. I started writing down every single thing I spent my money on. Still do. Talk about an eye opener. This opened my eyes to where my money went. It also allowed me to design a plan to move in a different direction. Now, there are some things you just have to spend money on, like food, shelter and new golf clubs (yes, really!). And some things you can do without, like that new tablet PC or the latest smart phone. The point I'm making is, know where your money goes and why. This will help you use your money in a smarter way.

Number Three: Where you live and work.

This is a tough one. Because it goes back to the money issue again. However, this is a mindset as well. Did you take the first job offered or the first house or apartment you looked at? Did you pick a neighborhood or occupation because you liked it or was it because someone said "I think you may be good at it or I could see you living there?" Be honest with yourself here. Would you have chosen it for yourself? Are you living the same lifestyle as your parents, friends and family? Did you want something different and were too afraid to step out of that life track and into one that better suited your soul? I too walked this path for many years. Attempting to live up to the expectations of those around me, instead of the ones I set for myself, was seemingly easier, but ultimately didn't bring true contentment. The art of working for yourself demands of you that you do what suits you. You find and set your own benchmarks of achievement. Run your own race and blaze your own path. It's fine to follow some of the footsteps that have lit the path ahead. For those with the desire to work for themselves, there will come a time when you must find your own way and create something of your own design and desire. Look at your list. I'm sure there will be some things that stand out as to who you want to be, where you want to live and how you want to work. Start moving in that direction and you won't be disappointed and watch everything you need for the journey find its way to you or you will find it along the way.

<u>Number Four:</u> Do a Personal Inventory.

This by far may be the toughest thing you must do in embracing the art of working for yourself. Taking stock of you, your friends and family is critical to your success. Let's face it, nice guys don't hang out with thugs and mean girls don't hang out with Cinderella. It's true what they say, "Birds of a feather, flock together." This brings me to family. They say you can't choose your family. Well, there is some truth to this. However, you don't live with them and you can set your watch on how much time you want to spend with them. The same goes for other things and people in your life. Think about the people you know and ask, whom do you tend to roll your eyes at the thought of having them in your presence. What events or obligations and the thought of attending them make your palms sweaty? Why invite what you don't like or want into your life? If it is something or someone you'd rather not spend time with "Say no thank you." Feel free to use me as an "out." Tell them, Gerald doesn't think you should do or spend time with…" There it's done. And if they ask who is this Gerald guy, share a copy of this book with them and tell them to address their feedback right over here! Emotional clutter I would put up there with visual noise. You spend so much time thinking about it, it robs you of the energy to think of the things you'd rather be doing. Choose your friends and the things you invite into your life with care and intention. Now I know this sounds like common sense but, we seldom exercise it in an effort to be politically correct.

Now, yes there are some things you should do to be kind and support others. However, when it takes on the appearance of agony on your part to keep it up. Call a halt immediately and move on.

And stay away from the "Ain't it awful club." Where there is smoke there's fire. People who complain hang out with others who do as well, and they are always looking for new members.

Find those who are doing the things that are on your list. There you will find kindred spirits who will nourish you and lift you up.

<u>Number Five:</u> Das Plan – Who, What, Where, When and Why.

It's time to start crafting your plan to begin the art of working for yourself. Begin with the "Who." Who is going on the journey with you? You will not be undertaking this alone. Because you are re-creating your life, you will be probably affecting others indirectly and they may challenge you on a few things as well and their understanding of who you are becoming.

Next comes the "What." What exactly are you doing and will you be going to work for yourself? Are you starting a business, changing careers or merely redesigning how you work so you get more out of it? It's all in the "what."

The "Where" part is tricky because when people begin to change, the things they look at also change. It can be like looking through high powered binoculars. Things get a whole lot clearer as you begin to see exactly what and where it is you want to go.

Now, "When" is easy because taking action is usually a present moment thing. But, sometimes it's like going to the airport before you go on vacation. You have to wait for your plane to arrive before you can board your flight to the "Bahamas."

And last but not least "Why" is the most important piece to this puzzle. Why is the reason behind all of this change to begin with. Why are you doing all of this? Something was the catalyst that sparked this journey. Find this oh so important and specific reason. I guarantee you there was a moment of "aha" and that changed your potential trajectory. It now becomes about honoring that "realization." Search your <u>Dream List</u> and I guarantee you'll find that first thing that got the ball rolling down this path. There is meaning in living the art of working for yourself. Find it. You'll know what you do.

So, just like any plan, you must write this down. It doesn't matter if it is in the form of a story, a huge long list or on post it note (my favorite, seriously). Then you must read it. As often as necessary to become familiar with it. It should be so ingrained in your mind and memory that if anyone were to ask you what you are doing, it will flow from your mind to your mouth easily.

I have occasionally run into someone with that much clarity. It's refreshing and passionate. You will begin to feel pretty darn focused as your plan begins to take shape. You probably won't be able to wipe the smile off of your face either. Nor will anyone else for that matter. So write on!

<u>Number Six:</u> Do Absolutely NOTHING!

There I said it! Do nothing. It's almost like saying a bad word to some people. Give yourself permission to do nothing. You see most of us are busy, just to say we are busy. If you think I'm wrong, listen the next time you ask someone what they are doing. They will give you a lot of little things they have to do. I'll get to the time management thing later. It's a shame that we can't say, "I'm doing nothing. Better yet, I'm resting."

Let's face it. We are over stimulated by television, our phones, tablets and social media. We have over-scheduled our lives beyond recognition. It's non-stop. Have you ever thought of taking a break? I did. Actually, mine was more like a break-down, which is what most of us probably encounter at some point. Some of us are holding it together better than others and some of us just have mini-break downs in the form of yelling, screaming, crying or the silent treatment towards our loved ones--all in an attempt to get some down time. I did my first test run over a major holiday (about two and a half weeks). I fell completely off the grid so to speak. No phones, no TV or social media, practically no luxuries, not even a book. Okay, I took a shower every day but that's it. I even limited talking to a minimum. Guess what happened? NOTHING! The world didn't fall off of its axis. My friends still loved me. I just took a much needed break for myself and came back fresher than ever.

Giving yourself permission to do nothing is huge. Because you begin to think about and do only the things you want to do. When I came through my time off the grid. I looked at the things I did and the things I like to do and began to make better choices. You'll be amazed at how this will work for you. Now, here's a word of caution. It's very easy to get swept back into your old ways. This is what your <u>Dream List</u> and <u>Das Plan</u> is for. Keep them close. You may even think of a few things to add while you are "doing nothing." I plan on doing this at least once a year to clear my head. Probably not over a major holiday though. It freaks out your friends and family. Then they start asking you if you've had too much to drink or is the potato salad bad. All of which aren't good.

<u>Number Seven:</u> Time Management and Box Checking.

How much time do you waste? Yes, this is a real question. I had someone ask me this one day. I said "oh not much, I stay pretty busy." I mean. I never wasted time at all. Listen, I was the poster boy for getting stuff done. Actually, not really. I read a book not too long ago. Author of "The Four Hour Work Week" Tim Ferriss called it doing "W4WS (Work for Work Sake)." Well, that's what I was doing. I was great at looking busy. Until I read this book. Then, I did something unheard of in the business world. I cleaned off my desk and soon found out how busy I wasn't. I just gave the appearance of busy-ness. Which is where I think the majority of us are.

Think about this. Why is it that the day before you go away on vacation you have the clarity, focus and drive to clear your email inbox, clean your house, change the oil in your car, get your tires rotated and wash and fold all the laundry in the house before you walk out of the door? It's amazing. I know, I used to be that guy. Now, I ask myself am I doing W4WS.

In embracing the art of working for yourself you must do the work that must be done and no more. I know this sounds rather limiting and off-kilter but think about it. When you are doing everything that must be done it leaves little room for waste. It's being efficient and effective. If you respect your time and your work others will too.

Also, use your technology to your advantage. I only check email twice a day. I also leave my email address on my cell phone voicemail so if you miss me in one realm you can get to me in another. Then I can choose when and how I respond--If you choose to leave a message. The way I look at it. I have voicemail for a reason. Sometimes, I don't want to be that in touch. When I'm at the beach watching the waves, I'm at the beach watching the waves and don't want to be disturbed.

When I first started this practice I felt a little guilty because society makes us think we should be at everyone's beck and call. So not true. Manage your own time and you'll be amazed at how much time you have to do anything you want.

Number Eight: Eliminate and Purge

I'll never forget the day I went to the "Goodwill" with a truck load full of stuff from my basement and garage after the end of a long relationship.

One word of advice; don't wait that long (I needed a big truck). It was actually really nice stuff. Like the boom box that played cassette's (I didn't even own cassette's anymore) and shoe's I had only worn twice because I swore I was going to buy some pants to go with them (what can I say, I like clothes). I love the Goodwill, Salvation Army and other things like yard sales. I'm always amazed at what I find. There is truth in the saying: "One man's junk is another man's treasure."

It felt so good to let go of the things in my life that I no longer needed. The things that held memories good and bad. It was like closing a chapter of my life and getting ready for something new. The art of working for yourself will be something new for most of us. However, there are some things that we must let go of to make room for the next chapter in our lives. Material and mental. We start things and feel we must finish them, when nothing could be further from the truth. Bad food is just bad food. You don't finish it do you? Well, why should you hold on to things that you don't want? Oh, I get it. It's the finish everything on your plate or you won't get any dessert thing, huh? Well, I'll let you in on a little secret. You can have your dessert for breakfast if you want (or cold pizza if you like it!).

And all of you hoarders aren't off of the hook either. You are never going to read all of those articles in that stack of magazines on your bookshelf dating back to 1997. To me this is what I call visual noise. It takes up space in my field of vision so much so that I can't stop thinking about it because it's there in my line of sight reminding me that I haven't done anything with it. Which takes me back to how I developed my <u>6 Month Rule</u>. So what, you never got to finishing or reading all of those articles.

The art of working for yourself demands that you are more efficient with your time and more selective with what you allow yourself to do and the speed at which you take action.

Here's is a fair trade off. As you are throwing the magazines away. Tear out the articles you want and trash the rest. The stack is now smaller and you won't feel guilty when you then toss it away. I learned this trick from a fellow traveler on a flight to New York. I noticed her tearing out a couple of articles from a magazine as the plane landed. I asked her why she did this after paying for this great magazine. She said "I rarely ever read an entire magazine. I don't pay too much attention to the ads so I take the parts I want and leave the rest for someone else to enjoy." You never know, they might only want the magazine for the ads. Since that day, I've done the same whenever I buy a magazine.

The same philosophy applies to anything else in my life. When I no longer have use for it. I let it go or don't finish it. Don't get me wrong, I don't believe in wasting anything.

That's why I've become more selective with what I allow into, my life. Because as you begin to eliminate and purge things, what you spend your time and money on matters even more because you begin to see the potential for waste, and wasting time and money are things that keep you from mastering the art of working for yourself.

Number Nine: Time to run your life.

When I started this journey. I didn't think I had control of much of anything in my life. Knowing what I know today, I know I control everything in my life. I also made a commitment to give 100% to everything I do and touch. From connecting with friends and family to the work I choose to do. It has to be done with all of my energy. Anything less is not worth attempting. The art of working for yourself allows you to be 100% engaged in everything you do because it is exactly what you want to do 100% of the time. Thus, giving you the energy and focus to be 100% present and always give 100% of what you have.

Think about it this way. When on those odd occasions you end up doing something other than what you want to do. Do you really give 100%? If you don't then you know why and if you do you also know why. Either way you've chosen to give the effort that speaks to how you feel about yourself and how you work.

You now have the foundation for a new way of life, a new way of working and being. They say the journey of one thousand miles begins with the first step. All the answers you need are inside of you. Listen to your heart and focus your mind and your journey will be amazing. In the end, what you do matters as much as what you think about what you do. This is the "Art of Working For Yourself."

"Alone we can do so little, together we can do so much."

– Helen Keller

Acknowledgments and Appreciation

They say that we are the sum total of our experiences. Whether by accident or on purpose I've probably made every mistake in the book and even some that aren't in the book. Nevertheless here I am. I once read a quote from Dr. Seuss that said "Don't cry because it happened, smile because it did." (actually I changed it just a little, but you get my point) There is no way on earth to acknowledge everyone who has had an impact on my life and I am forever grateful for such a creative and inspiring universe that has given me the vision to create this body of work to share with the world.

Let me begin with my parents Howard and Patricia Grinter-- who showed me what love and hard work really mean. Next, I would like to thank Sue McCabe for sharing a whole new world with me I never knew possible. My brother and sister Bill and Christine - who have always loved me no matter what and have shared so much laughter with me until I've had a splitting headache. I love you guys. Also, a very special smile of love to my cousins, aunts and uncles who have also been an important part of my life and helped shape who I have become. Thank you for the bottom of my heart.

I wish I had enough time and words to mention all of the teachers and mentors who were there when the student was ready and have lit the path before me, sometimes even dragging me kicking and screaming. Ms. Mullin whose grasshopper pie and afternoon stories made me want learn how to be a great storyteller, Coach Bob Fowl who also taught me how to run my own race no matter what the conditions are (even in a thunderstorm). Stanley O. McNaughton, who shared a smile with me and taught me how to share it with the world. The Champions Club who taught me what business is all about. Thank you for allowing me to be a part of something greater than myself. Tuesday afternoons with Deborah Drake and her "Reticent Writing" family who helped me allow my heart and words to connect. To Don Burrows, sir, thank you for the "so what's" and the push to keep searching inside myself to find the meatball. I love you man. Messha Martin I will never forget you. Thank you for pushing me off of the rock.

There are also a few authors and icons who have had a major impact on life and have allowed me to find the path I now walk. This goes as follows and in no certain order: Richard Branson, Dr. Deepak Chopra, Dr. Wayne Dyer, Zig Ziglar, Tony Robbins, Seth Godin, Tim Ferriss, Harvey MacKay, Napoleon Hill, Wallace

D. Wattles, Robert Greene, Jeffrey Gittomer, Dr. Steven C. Covey, Brian Tracey, Ted Turner, T. Boone Pickens, Donald Trump, Tom Hopkins, Jack Canfield, Warren Buffett, Mark Cuban and the countless other entrepreneurs, business leaders and inspirational acquaintances who have helped me understand what it means and how to appreciate the art of working for yourself.

Last and not least, I want to thank "you" for reading "The Art of Working for Yourself." I have given this book every ounce of my heart and soul in the hope that you embrace the art of working for yourself and create the life you've always imagined. Thank you. Until we meet again. Be well.

"Life isn't about finding yourself. Life is about creating yourself."- George Bernard Shaw

The Blacklist: Undercover Reading

I realize there are so many books and resources out there that will inspire and amaze you I couldn't end this book without at least putting you on the path of a couple that have helped me. These books I urge you to read now that you understand that you should always work for yourself, no matter who you work for. They will become the mortar to the bricks of the foundation you are creating.

The 4-Hour Workweek - Tim Ferriss

(thefourhourworkweek.com)

Tim Ferriss does a brilliant job of creating the blueprint for lifestyle redesign and giving you ideas, case studies and resources that will inspire anyone looking to always work for themselves.

Think and Grow Rich – Napoleon Hill

(naphill.org)

What can I say, this book is timeless and is probably the foundation for anyone who is ready to look inside themselves and examine those limiting beliefs and behaviors they want to change.

The Success Principles - Jack Canfield

(jackcanfield.com/products)

I found this book several years ago and I read it about three times and even put it on my iPod. You may remember Jack Canfield's - "Chicken Soup for the Soul." Well to me "Success Principles" is the perfect follow up to that book and is a step by step process in understanding of what being successful truly takes.

E-Myth Revisited - Michael Gerber

(e-myth.com)

I love this book. As a business owner I believe it is a must read for anyone who owns a business. Michael Gerber breaks down how to design your business to practically run automatically and how to work on your business and not in it.

48 Laws of Power - Robert Greene

(Amazon.com)

I recommend this book for one reason only. It is an excellent case study in human behavior and how to recognize some of the forces in life that may have been invisible to you and often made you wonder why things happened that way the do and why some people act the way they do.

The Power of "Now" – Eckhart Tolle

(eckharttolle.com)

This book is profound in its writing and process because there is nothing more important than right "now." Start where you are because that's all we ever have. You can't change the past and the future doesn't exist. Become present in your life and watch it take shape.

These books are a start to the process of working for yourself and I'm pleased to have you on this journey with me.

"The greatest danger for most of us is not that our aim is too high and we miss it, but our aim is too low and we reach it."

– Michelangelo

Photo Credit For
The Art Of Working For Yourself
Courtesy of Fotolia

Front and Back Cover. ArTo
14. Vetal
26. Galian Barskaya
35. Victor Zastal'skiy
45. Giordano Aita
56. Olly
64. Olly
74. Alexander Trinitatov
83. Viktor Kuran
91. Dundanim
102. Alexander Yakovlev
121. Jakub Cypek
125. Magann
130. Txasko

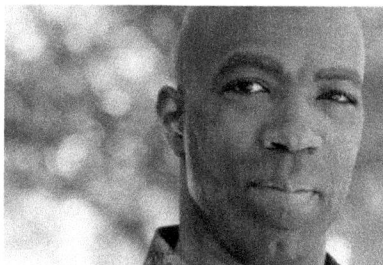

ABOUT THE AUTHOR

Gerald Grinter is an entrepreneur/business owner who started an insurance agency from scratch and ten years later sold his business for more than he could have ever imagined, which is pretty impressive when you consider that he did not set out to build a business to sell. He was astonished when three different larger agencies offered to purchase his insurance agency.

A funny thing happened when he reinvented his agency after splitting from his business partner, he took full advantage of technology so as to go as paperless as possible and systematized / streamline everything he could. As it turned out, he had unintentionally created a valuable asset that would make money while not being at all dependent upon him as the source of that money. E-Myth author Michael Gerber advised his entrepreneurial clients : "Go to work ON your business, not IN your business." That's precisely what he did, and in March 2010 he sold his agency and never looked back.

Now as a full-fledged entrepreneur and business mentor he began looking at the world through that lens, he began seeing needs going unmet, and packaged himself as the solution to those needs. He became a volunteer mentor at the Non-Profit Micro-Lending organization Washington CASH (Community Alliance for Self Help). Ever a believer in technology and having identified the need to provide and understand e-services to my existing mentees who all had e-businesses, he created YouGoGirlSolutions.com to extend his effectiveness by offering a range of on-line business education and support to other women business owners. He got to help his mentees business owners write their business and marketing plans, develop and implement their new sales strategies, and was treated to a ringside seat as new businesses were born and took their first new steps. He now co-mentors and supports fifteen new business owners and eagerly awaits his next inspiration.

The Art of Working for Yourself

www.ingramcontent.com/pod-product-compliance
Lightning Source LLC
Chambersburg PA
CBHW071555040426
42452CB00008B/1183